# INVESTMENT VA

## LEARN PROVEN METHODS FOR DETERMINING ASSET VALUE AND TAKING THE RIGHT INVESTING DECISIONS

**Descrierea CIP a Bibliotecii Naţionale a României**

**Investment Valuation. Learn Proven Methods For Determining Asset Value And Taking The Right Investing Decisions**. – Bucharest: My Ebook Publishing House, 2018
    ISBN 978-606-983-629-3

# INVESTMENT VALUATION
## LEARN PROVEN METHODS FOR DETERMINING ASSET VALUE AND TAKING THE RIGHT INVESTING DECISIONS

My Ebook Publishing House
Bucharest, 2018

# CONTENTS

# INTRODUCTION

*I want to use this medium to thank and congratulate you for downloading this book **"Investment Valuation: Learn Proven Methods For Determining Asset Value And Taking The Right Investing Decisions"***

Valuation is at the core of any investment choice, regardless of whether that choice is a purchase, offer or hold. Be that as it may, the valuing of many assets has turned into a more complex assignment in present day markets, particularly after the current money related emergency. Keeping in mind the end goal to be effective at this undertaking, you should have a firm comprehension of the best possible valuation strategies.

Each benefit, cash correlated and moreover real, has a worth. The way to efficiently contributing in and dealing with these benefits lies in understanding what the value is as well as the origins of the cost. Any asset can be valued, yet a few resources are less demanding to an incentive than others and the points of interest of valuation will shift from case to case. In this way, the valuation of an offer of a real estate property will require diverse data and take after a fantastic organization in comparison to the valuation of a traded on an open market stock. What is astounding, in any case, isn't the distinctions in valuation systems crosswise over resources, however the level of similitude in essential standards. There is unquestionably vulnerability related to valuation. Frequently that vulnerability originates from the asset being valued. However, the valuation model may add to that vulnerability.

Presently overhauled entirely and refreshed to reflect changing economic situations, this third version thoroughly acquaints investment experts and understudies with the scope of valuation models accessible and how to pick the correct model for any given resource valuation situation. This version incorporates valuation strategies for an entire host of real alternatives, start-up firms, unpredictable resources, bothered organizations and private value, and real estate.

A propose of sound investing is that an investor does not pay more for an asset than its value. This announcement may appear to be coherent and self-evident, yet it is overlooked and rediscovered sooner or later in each age and each market. Discernments might be the only things that are in any way meaningful when the asset is a depiction of a figure. However, investors don't (and ought not) purchase most resources for stylish or passionate reasons; financial resources are gained from the sources of

8

income expected on them. Thus, the impression of value must be going down by reality, which suggests that the cost paid for any asset ought to mirror the sources of income that it is relied upon to produce. The models of valuation depicted in this book endeavor to relate value to the level and expected the development of these sources of income.

There are numerous zones in valuation where there is space for difference, including step by step instructions to gauge absolute value and to what extent it will take at costs to acclimate to genuine value. However, there is one point on which there can be no difference. Resource costs can't be advocated by just utilizing the contention that there will be different investors around eager to pay a higher cost later on.

*Thanks again for downloading this book and I hope you enjoy it.*

policies, processes, or directions contained within is the solitary and utter responsibility of the recipient reader. Under no circumstances will any legal responsibility or blame be held against the publisher for any reparation, damages, or monetary loss due to the information herein, either directly or indirectly.

Respective authors own all copyrights not held by the publisher.

The information herein is offered for informational purposes solely, and is universal as so. The presentation of the information is without contract or any type of guarantee assurance.

The trademarks that are used are without any consent, and the publication of the trademark is without permission or backing by the trademark owner. All trademarks and brands within this book are for clarifying purposes only and are the owned by the owners themselves, not affiliated with this document.

# CHAPTER ONE

## APPROACHES TO INVESTMENT VALUATION

Market analyst utilizes an extensive variety of facsimiles to value resources practically speaking, extending from the easy to the refined. These prototypes often make altogether different presumptions about evaluating. However, they do have some natural qualities too, and they can be ordered in lengthier rapports.

Taking everything into account positions, there is more than one way to deal with valuation. The to begin with, *marked down* income estimate, transmits the value of an asset for the contemporary importance of anticipated future cash flows on that benefit. The subsequent, comparative valuation, evaluates the significance of investment by taking a gander at the estimating of 'equivalent' resources concerning a standard variable, for example, profit, book value, cash flows or deals. The third, *unexpected claim valuation*, utilizes choice evaluating models to quantify the number of benefits that share alternative attributes. Approximately of these benefits are exchanged financial resources like merits, and more or less of these alternatives are not merchandized and depend on real resources – activities, licenses and oil saves are cases. The last is often known as real preferences. At hand, there are noteworthy contrasts in results, contingent on which methodology is utilized. One of the destinations in this book is to clarify the explanations behind such disparities in value crosswise over various models and to help in picking the right model to use for a particular errand.

While valuing an organization as a standard concern, there are over two ways for ultimate valuation strategies utilized by industry professionals:

- DCF investigation or analysis,
- Relative Valuation and
- Claim Valuation

These remain the utmost widely recognized strategies for valuation used as a part of investment keeping the money, value investigates, private value, corporate development, fusions, and purchases leveraged purchases and most regions of the back.

### *Outline of Valuation Methods*

While esteeming an industry or resource, there are more than two (three exactly) general groupings that each encompass their exacting strategies. The Cost Methodology takes a gander at what it charges to amass a product, and this technique isn't much of the time utilized by back mavens to rate an organization as an age long concern. Afterward is the Market Tactic, this is a form of qualified valuation and much of the time utilized as a part of the industry. It incorporates Analogous Analysis Guide

Transactions. At long last, the *marked down* income (DCF) approach is a form of congenital assessment and is the most point by point and thorough way to deal with assessment validating.

- **Discounted Cashflow Valuation**

Discounted Cash Flow (DCF) study is an inherent value approach where an expert forecasts the business' unlevered free income into the future and markdown it back to today at the association's Weighted Average Cost of Captial (WACC).

A DCF investigation is performed by building a financial model in Excel and requires a broad measure of detail and examination. It is the most itemized of the three methodologies, requires the most suppositions and often delivers the highest value. In any case, the effort required for setting up a DCF model will likewise often result in the most accurate valuation. A DCF show enables the examiner to forecast value given various situations, and even perform an affectability investigation.

For more prominent organizations, the DCF value is usually a complete of-the-parts examination, where several specialty units are displayed separately and included.

While *marked down* income valuation is unique of all the three methods for drawing closer valuation and most valuations done in reality are virtual valuations, we will contend that the aforementioned is the establishment on which other valuation styles are manufactured. To do comparative valuation fittingly, we have to comprehend the basics of *discounted* income survey. To relate alternative estimating simulations to value resources, we often need in any case a **Discounted income valuation**. This is the reason such an extensive amount this book centers around Discounted income valuation. Any individual who comprehends its essentials will have the capacity to examine also, utilize alternate methodologies. In this area, we will think about the premise of this slant, a philosophical method of reasoning for *discounted* income valuation and an analysis of the distinctive sub-ways to deal with *discounted* income valuation.

### *Discounted Cashflow Evaluation*

This methodology has its establishment in the extant value administer, where the rate of any source is the extant value of estimated future cash flows that the asset produces.

$t=n$ CFt Value $= \sum (1+r)t$
$t=1$

*where,*

$n$ = *Life of the asset*

$CFt$ = *Cashflow in period t*

$r$ = *Discount rate replicating the audaciousness of the valued cash flows.*

The cash flows will change from a resource to resource - profits for stocks, vouchers (premium) Furthermore, the surface assessment for bonds and after-impose cashflows for an existent task. The markdown percentage will be a component of the peril of the assessed cashflows, with sophisticated rates for more hazardous resources and lower prices for more secure ventures. You can in actuality consider *marked down* income valuation on a gamut. Toward one side of the range, you have the sans default nil voucher bond, with an ensured trade stream out what's to come. Reducing this income at the less-risky rate should yield the value of the security. Somewhat auxiliary up the range are corporate securities where the money streams appear as vouchers, and there is default hazard.

These securities can be valued by reducing the average money streams at a loan fee that mirrors the default hazard. Ascending the hazard stepping stool, we affect values, where there are expected money streams with significant vulnerability to the desire.

- **Relative Valuation**

Relative valuation usually referred to as valuation utilizing products is the idea of contrasting the cost of a benefit with the market value of comparative resources. In the field of securities investment, the thought has prompted critical functional instruments, which could probably spot valuing oddities. These devices have in this manner end up instrumental in empowering examiners and investors to settle on essential choices on resource designation.

While we tend to concentrate most on discounted income valuation, while talking about valuation, the reality is that most valuations are relative valuations. The value of most resources, from the house you purchase to the stocks that you invest in, depending on how comparable resources are estimated in the market put. We start this area with a reason for relative valuation, proceed onward to consider the underpinnings of the model and after that think about normal variations in relative valuation

In equities, the concept isolates into two zones – one relating to singular investments and the other two lists.

### Singular equities

The most widely recognized strategy for singular equities depends on contrasting specific financial proportions or products, for example, the cost to book value, cost to profit, EV/EBITDA, and so on., of the value being referred to those of its companions. This kind of approach, which is well known as a critical device in the financial business, is for the most part measurable and in light of historical information.

### Value indexes

For a value index the above bombs mostly because it is hard to amass records into peer gatherings. Thus, relative valuation here is for the most part done by looking at a national or industry stock index's performance to the monetary and market basics of the related business or nation.

Those basics may incorporate GDP development, financing cost, and expansion forecasts, and also income development, among others. This style of correlation is mainstream among rehearsing business analysts in their endeavor to defend the associations between the value markets and the economy.

The national value index is not entirely pertinent in this regard because of the proportion of multinational organizations recorded in most domestic stock markets.

**Bonds**

When valuing a bond, the relationship is referred to will be evaluated relative to a benchmark, more often than not a Government bond. Here, the "required return" - in fact, the vital development or

YTM - on the bond is resolved in light of the bond's Credit rating relative to administration security with comparable growth. The better the nature of the bond, the littler the spread between its YTM and the YTM of the benchmark.

- **Contingent Claim Valuation**

Contingent claim valuation utilizes alternative estimating models to gauge the value of assets that share choice qualities.

Let's begin with finite markets. A market is referred to as *finite* if the example space and time are discrete and finite. Finite markets have the preferred standpoint of keeping away from specific issues that happen in markets with infinite parts.

The second segment expands the concept from the finite markets to consistent time, constant state markets. We overlook the re-inference of all the measurable outcomes in the logical world because the instinct is unaltered, the detail of the proofs enormously increments.

However, we do build up two outcomes after that a significant part of the material in the rest of the sections depends. Initially, the presence of an exceptional identical martingale measure in a market suggests nonattendance of arbitrage. Second, given such a likelihood measure, a claim can be mainly imitated by a self-financing exchanging procedure with the end goal that the investment expected to execute the system corresponds to the contingent desire of the emptied future value of the claim under the martingale measure. Therefore, the cost of a claim has an essential portrayal in the wording of a willingness and an emptying numeraire resource.

In a sans arbitrage market, it can be demonstrated that culmination is proportional to the presence of a unique martingale measure. We work with the entire market setting. If the market is inadequate, the martingale measure is never again one of a kind, suggesting that arbitrage can't value the claims utilizing a duplicating, self-financing exchanging methodology.

As earlier said. There exist three ultimate, however not entirely unrelated, ways to deal with valuation. The to start with is discounted capital valuation, where cash flows are discounted at a hazard steady rebate rate to land at a gauge of value. The examination should be possible solely from the point of view of value investors, by marking down anticipated that cash flows would value at the cost of value, or it should be possible from the perspective of all claim holders in the firm, by scoring down expected that cash flows would be the firm at the weighted reasonable cost of capital. The second is relative valuation, where the value of the value in a firm depends on the evaluating of practically identical firms relative to income, book value, cash flows or auctions. The third is contingent claim valuation, where a benefit with the qualities of choice is valued utilizing a decision evaluating the model. There ought to be a place for each of the devices accessible to any expert intrigued by valuation.

# CHAPTER TWO

## UNDERSTANDING FINANCIAL STATEMENTS

These are account sheets for all business. Regardless if you are another investor, an entrepreneur, a chief, a non-profit administrator, an official or merely endeavoring to monitor your funds, you have to see how to peruse, break down, and make financial reports, hence you can get a full and exact regarding how much cash there is, how copious arrears is unsettled, the wage coming in every month, and the expenses.

It is essential, therefore, that we comprehend the standards representing these statements by taking a gander at four inquiries:

- How valuable are the benefits of a firm? The benefits of a firm can come in a few forms – resources with long lives, for example, land and structures, resources with shorter lives such inventory, and impalpable resources that still deliver incomes for the firm, for example, licenses furthermore, trademarks.

- How did the firm raise the funds to back these assets? In gaining these benefits, firms can utilize the funds of the proprietors (value) or borrowed cash (obligation), and the blend is prone to change as the chattels era.

- How profitable are these assets? A decent investment, we contended, is one that makes a return more noteworthy than the obstacle rate. To assess whether the investments that a firm has officially made are significant investments, we have to evaluate what returns we are building on these investments.

- How much vulnerability (or hazard) is implanted in these assets? While we have not straightforwardly gone up against the issue of risk yet, evaluating how much weakness there is in existing investments and the suggestions for a firm is obviously an initial step.

## The Almanac Report

A significant number of the pecuniary accounts you have to comprehend an organization are confined to the almanac report. This will provide you an inkling of the almanac report, how you can ask for unique for an impending stock, and why you have to choose it on the off chance that you anticipate breaking down financial reports. Get acquainted with the almanac statement...

## 10K and the Financial Statements

The 10K is an exceptional accumulation of financial statements that an organization is required to document with the Securities and Exchange Commission. It incorporates substantially more information, much of the time, than the almanac report.

## How to Declaim and Analyze the Stability (Often referred to as balance) Sheet

Of the three critical financial accounts, the poise sheet is the one that gives a depiction in a stretch of what is obsessed (investment), what is owed (debts), and what is left finished (total assets or book value). This well-ordered manual for the balance sheet will walk you through each line, clarify what everything means, and demonstrate to you a few things to search for when perusing financial statements. Crossing more than thirty-seven pages, it resembles a free school course reading planned entirely for new investors that have no foundation in back. Figure out how to peruse and comprehend the balance sheet

## Reading and Analyzing the Income Account

The second of the three pecuniary reports are the income articulation. In some cases, called the revenue and loss, the income articulation indicates your income, costs, and as missing finished a short time later (revenue, or income). The income edict is essential for the reason that you can utilize it, alongside the equilibrium expanse, to ascertain the arrival you are procuring on your speculation if it's a condo building you possess, an independent company you manage, or a possible stock you are thinking about purchasing or offering.

## *Utilizing the Financial Statements to Analyze Financial Percentages*

The principle motivation to figure out how to peruse financial statements is with the goal that you could ascertain economic proportions. Economic proportions allow you distinguish how an organization is getting along, how lucrative it is, whether management is assuming excessively obligation, potential issues investors could look not far off, and significantly more. Beginning figuring out how to ascertain financial proportions ...

## *Looking Further than the Financial Accounts*

Now and then, you have to look further than the monetarist avowals to comprehend what is going on and the perilous undermining your investments. Envision, for a minute, yourself taking a gander at the economic reports of a stallion and surrey producer in the mid-twentieth century. Regardless of how modest the business showed up, you wouldn't have any desire to purchase stocks for the reason that the vehicle was working to pulverize the whole industry soon.

### *Ace Forma Financial Statements*

On the off chance that you read the yearbook report and you see something many refer to as "Expert Forma" reports, you be duty-bound to discontinue, genuinely cogitate whether or not you can believe the management. Genius forma implies that the fiscal reports don't conform to the GAAP guidelines.

Source: https://www.thebalance.com/guide-to-understanding-financial-statements-357512

# CHAPTER THREE

## THE BASICS OF RISK

Valuation risk is the monetarist risk that an asset is overestimated and is worth not as much as expected when it ripens or is sold. Factors adding to valuation risk can incorporate inadequate information, market unsteadiness, financial displaying vulnerabilities and poor information examination by the general population in charge of deciding the value of the benefit. This risk can be a worry for investors, loan specialists, financial regulators and other individuals engaged with the financial markets. Overvalued assets can make misfortunes for their proprietors and prompt reputational risks; conceivably affecting FICO assessments, subsidizing costs and the management structures of business organizations.

Valuation risks concern each phase of the exchange preparing and investment management chain. From the front office, to back office, circulation, resource management, private riches and advisory administrations. This is especially valid for assets that have low liquidity and are not effortlessly tradable in broad daylight exchanges. Moreover, issues related to valuation risks go past the firm itself. With straight-through preparing and algorithmic exchanging, information and valuations must stay synchronized among the members of the trade handling chain. The executing scene, prime brokers, overseer banks, finance administrators, exchange operators and review share documents electronically and attempt to mechanize such procedures, raising potential risks identified with information management and valuations.

To relieve this risk, it is crucial to give straightforwardness and guarantee the respectability and consistency of the information, models, and procedures used to process and report counts inside valuations for all members.

### Not Comparing

Contrasting an establishment's stock with that of its rivals is one-way value investors evaluate their potential investments. Notwithstanding, organizations vary in their secretarial approaches in means that are impeccably lawful. When you're looking at one organization's P/E proportion to another's, you need to ensure that EPS has been situated figural in a similar path for the two organizations. Additionally, you won't have the capacity to analyze organizations from various ventures.

### Focusing Your Calculations on the Wrong Numbers

Since value investing choices are halfway in light of an examination of financial statements, it is essential that you perform these counts correctly. Utilizing the wrong numbers, showing the incorrect computation or influencing a mathematical grammatical mistake to can bring about constructing an investment choice in light of broken information. You may then make a poor investment or pass up a significant opportunity for an extraordinary one. On the off chance that you aren't yet sure about your capacity to peruse and analyze financial statements and reports, continue considering these subjects and don't put any trades until the point when you're genuinely prepared.

### *Sitting above Extraordinary Gains or Losses*

A few years, organizations encounter bizarrely great misfortunes or additions from occasions, for example, cataclysmic events, corporate rebuilding or outlandish claims and will report these on the income articulation under a name, for example, "extraordinary thing – pick up" or "extraordinary thing – misfortune." When making your counts, it is essential to expel these financial oddities from the condition to improve thought of how the organization may perform in an ordinary year. Notwithstanding, ponder these things and utilize your judgment. If an organization has an example of reporting the same extraordinary thing a seemingly endless amount of time, it won't be excessively remarkable. Additionally, if there are unexpected misfortunes quite a long time, this can be an indication that the organization is having financial issues. Extraordinary things should be strange and nonrecurring. Additionally, be careful an example of discounts.

### *Not Broadening horizons*
Ordinary investment shrewdness says that financing in single stocks can be a great risk methodology. Somewhat, we are educated to capitalize on various stocks or stock catalogs, so we have an introduction to a wide assortment of organizations and

financial sectors. Nonetheless, some investors trust that you know how to possess a broadened portfolio regardless of whether you just claim few stocks, given that you pick stocks that speak to various ventures and distinctive areas of the economy.

Then again, the authors of "Value Investing for Dummies," second. Ed., say that the more stocks you possess, the more noteworthy your odds are of accomplishing average market returns. They suggest investing in just a couple of organizations and inspecting them closely. Apparently, this exhortation accepts that you stand astonishing at picking victors, which might be a different kettle of fish, especially on the off chance that you are a value-financing tenderfoot.

### *Overlooking the Imperfections in Ratio Analysis*

Prior segments of this tutorial have examined the estimation of different financial proportions that assistance investors analyze an organization's economic well-being. The issue with fiscal balances is that they could remain computed in various ways. Here are a couple of elements that can influence the importance of these proportions:

- Most of them can be ascertained with before-charge or after-impose numbers.
- A few proportions give just unpleasant assessments.
- An organization's reported profit for every share (EPS) can change altogether contingent upon how "income" is characterized.

Organizations contrast in their book-keeping techniques, making it hard to analyze distinctive organizations of similar proportions precisely.

### Paying more than required

One significant peril in value investing is overpaying for a stock. Once you come up short on for a stock, you diminish the measure of cash you could mislay if the stock completes below par. The nearer you reimburse to the stock's fair value – or far more detestable, if you pay more than expected – the higher your possibility of not procuring cash or notwithstanding losing capital. Review that one of the ultimate standards of value endowing is to manufacture an edge of wellbeing into every one of your investments. This implies buying stocks at the cost of around 66% or not as much of their inherent value. Value investors need to risk as a diminutive investment as conceivable in possibly misconstrued assets, so they make an effort not to pay too much for investments.

### *Tuning in to Sentiments*

It is hard to disregard your feelings when settling on investment choices. Regardless of whether you pick isolates, the essential point of view while assessing numbers, dread and fervor may sneak in when the time to utilize some portion of your merited funds to buy a stock. More decisively, after you have obtained the share, you might be enticed to offer it if the value falls. You should recollect that being a valued stakeholder intends to stay away from the group attitude investment behaviors of purchasing when a stock's cost is going up and offering when it is dipping. Such action will wreck your profits.

### *Exchanging when it's right to do so*

Regardless of whether you do the whole *shebang* right in exploring and procurement your shares, your whole technique can go into disrepair on the off chance that you offer at the erroneous time. The wide of the mark time to sell is the point at which the marketplace is stable, and stock costs are falling substantially because stockholders are freezing, not on account of they are surveying the nature of the secret organizations they have capitalized on. One more terrible time to offer is the point at which a stock's value drops since its income has missed the mark regarding experts' desires.

The perfect time to offer your product is when dividends are overrated comparative to the organization's inherent value. Notwithstanding, once in a while a considerable modification in the organization or the business that brings down the organization's intrinsic value may likewise warrant a deal if you perceive misfortunes on the skyline. It could be precarious not to mistake these circumstances for general investor freeze. Additionally, if part of your outlay system includes passing riches to your beneficiaries, the exact time to offer might never be (at any rate for a quota of your selection).

Risk: In the investing world, the word reference meaning of risk is the possibility that an investment's actual return will be not the same as anticipated. Risk implies you have the likelihood of losing a few, or even all, of your original investment. Low levels of vulnerability (generally safe) are related to low potential returns. Elevated amounts of vulnerability (high risk) are correlated with high potential returns. The risk/return tradeoff is the balance between the want for the most minimal conceivable risk and the highest reasonable return. Investment risks can be separated into two categories: methodical and unsystematic.

Orderly Risk: Also known as "market risk" or "un-diversifiable risk," efficient risk is the vulnerability inalienable to the whole market or sliver. Likewise alluded to as instability, the calculated risk is the daily vacillations in a stock's cost. Instability is a measure of risk since it alludes to the behavior, or "demeanor," of your investment rather than the explanation behind this behavior. Since market development is the motivation behind why individuals can profit from stocks, unpredictability is ultimate for returns, and the more insecure the investment, the more shot there is that it will encounter an emotional alter in either course.

Unsystematic Risk: Also known as "particular risk," "diversifiable risk" or "leftover risk," this sort of vulnerability accompanies the organization or industry you invest in and can be decreased through divergence.

Credit or Default Risk: Credit risk is the risk that an organization or individual will be not able to pay the legally binding interest

Financial statements remain the essential wellspring of information for generally investors furthermore, examiners. There are contrasts, in any case, in how accounting and financial examination approach noting various critical inquiries regarding the firm. We inspect these contrasts in this part. Categorizing holdings into investments made efficiently (assets set up) and investments yet to be made (development assets), we contended that accounting statements give a generous measure of historical information about the former and next to **NO** about the last mentioned.

The emphasis on the original cost of assets set up (book value) in accounting statements can prompt critical contrasts between the expressed value of these assets and their market value. With development assets, accounting rules result in low or no benefits for assets created by inside research.

# CONCLUSION

*Thank you once again for downloading this book*

Valuation assumes a crucial part in numerous regions of fund - incorporate back, mergers and acquisitions and portfolio management. The models exhibited in this book will give a scope of instruments that examiners in every one of these zones will discover valuable, yet the preventative note sounded in this part bears rehashing. Valuation isn't a target work out, and any preconceptions and inclinations that an examiner conveys to the procedure will discover its way into the value.

*Having said that, if you enjoyed this book, then I will like to ask you for a favor, would you be kind enough to leave a review for this book? It will be greatly appreciated.*

*Thank You and Good luck*